# NATIONS AND PEOPLES

Judson Crews

CHERRY VALLEY EDITIONS

**Library of Congress Cataloging in Publication Data**

Crews, Judson.
    Nations and peoples.

    I.  Title.
PS3553.R47N3          811'.5'4          76-50426
ISBN 0-916156-19-2

NATIONS AND PEOPLE
LIVING ON THE EDGE OF A DEATH WISH

<u>In homage to Frantz Fanon</u>


I

Nations and people
   what was the timeless route
   which brought you to this hapless moment
   what mindless escapement
   will catapult you into the cauldron of eternity

You have risen up
   to the pinnacle of the sword
   on the black wings of the raven
   and on the white wings of the dove
   you have cut out the hearts
      of your strong enemies
   and you have cut out the bowels
      of your weak friends
You have risen up
   to the pinnacle of the sword
   on the soft flesh
      of forgotten people
 You have risen up
   against the face of God
   and against the backside of Satan
You command
   the pinnacle of the sword
   with a voice box orbitting outer space
   and with microphones implanted
      in the bedchamber of each confidant
      you have sworn to silence
You have risen up
   to the pinnacle of the sword
   on the mangled bodies
      of murdered opponents
   and upon the soft flesh of frightened yesmen

Nations and people
Living on the edge of a death wish

We voted for historical purpose
We voted for a clean mind
   and clean hands
We voted for a circumspect conscience
not to mention a reduction in taxes
And universal conscription
No beer sold on election day
   or Sunday prior to a quarter of three

Living on the edge of a death wish
   the precious burden
   the jewel of creation
   the creature that moves
   upon its belly
   silver slippers
   Bulltoven out of breath
   these dark breasts
   lightened with sweet talcum

Living on the edge of a death wish
   Oh, you kindly despots
   whose moral power is a wonder
   Whose ostentacious obeisance
   sparkles on every Sabbeth
   Who tea-totals on every week day
   Who posts an inspector of dirty minds
   at every border
Your cynical arm of power
   is an erect gun
   with live ammunition
And your name is Mammon
   That bitter lemon
   that once was your heart
   Dispenses bland unction
   as you bow and as you fart

Oh, the veils that have been
   ripped away
   Nations and continents
   Revealing the loathsome nakedness
   of scales and festering sores
   pustules of hate

Sebastian's wounds
and Bartholomew's stigmata
A burning pox
shamefully named for every nation
That loathsome nakedness
Where is the naked truth
that naked beauty
in all its white, or black
or olive splendour
Where are those straight thighs
and round breasts
those wellsprings of multiple
naked beauty

Living on the edge of a death wish
Wanting a chance to start over again
Wanting the tom-tom's return
to its drumming
Wanting the night as thick
as blood's brewing
Wanting the end as clear as the now
Wanting a search light beaming
the future
Wanting catastrophe on the "evils"
of others
Wanting the savage staked in the bush

There on the edge of a death wish
Wouldn't you know
that the world coming toward you
is a black-man's world in white-face
Wouldn't you know
there is lethal harm hidden
in all the hands reaching out toward you
Wouldn't you know
that the sweet talcumed butt by you
is surgery's new recompense
of sex-neuter sex-pot in mystical tandum
The fag is in drag
you just have to believe in
The clown with his frown
is the world upside down

The friendly old bugger is fixing
to eat you
That's the world coming out
to greet you

Living on the edge of a death wish
    Boils breaking the skin
    inflaming and swelling
    guns and knives
    Snakes bloating the belly
    when she squats to pee
    Hammurabi's soldiers
    five centuries away, or twenty-five
    on the edge of another continent
    Slumber will not be with them
    through this torrid dawn
    breaking over the bleak horizon
    the blistering coil of their
        taut flesh
    Morning and evening approaching
        night


II


Nations and people
    living on the edge of a death wish
    living by the law of the knife
    living upon the pinnacle of the sword

The body's brawn subverted
    for private gain
Man's harrowed hopes subverted
    for private gain
The brain's ingenuity subverted
    to the destruction
    of nations and people
    in the light of dawn's birth
    and in the quaking machinations
        of past midnight

You have killed with your
    lying teeth

with a knife fluid as talcum
and cool
with a hot sword molten
as bronze
You have killed with
an infinitude of diversions
with a fetish of logic
with a torque of technological
machinery
with the mastication of your
white teeth
and your scriptures of love
read to non-penitents
flayed at the stake

This is the putrid placenta
    fouling the womb
    corrupting the vagina

Living on the edge of a death wish
    Wanting twenty flags of twenty nations
    all planted in a row
    Wanting embargoes sanctioning
    all borders
    Wanting the ultimate
    in balance of payment
Wanting the ape inside
    repressed in the ape outside
    So the last savage is computerized
    with a tensile strength of
    XYZ plus
    and weak at that in
    the nincompoop
    Resisting balls of terror
    battering a lowering sky
    punctuated with supersonic whirlpools
    of black hope
    The computer centre is shorted out
    with the brass of his cods
    electrical by definition and circumstance
    and postmortem hallucination

Whose creditable heaven is it
    on the edge of a death wish
    Wanting the skin lighter
    and lighter
    Wanting the favours of princes
    and paupers
    Wanting the sanction of peace
    by the sword
    And a law of numbers
    Lebensnot
Whose bumper crop is babies
    dead and about to die
    --plowing them under
    to avert the sightless gaze
    starvation's glaze
    on their hollow eyes
    Lebensnot
    Next year's prospects
    are bigger, bigger
Oh, if the snake were craven
    If the sow, like a woman, went
    upon its belly
    If her gun were between her legs
    Who is the oppressor
    Who is Able without a name
    What the medicine bough
    golden and potent
    No ass less sweet
    than talcum's driven snow
    Tums for the tummy
    heavy bloating from too much eating

Living on the edge of a death wish
    Piss-ants and tadpoles
    in official helmets
    straddling flexible motorcycles
    at a high speed on a state occasion
How to dismantle the bureaucracy
    How to get new cannisters
    for the wham-wham bazookas
    How to keep the bidet spotless
    and sparkling for the new-girl-friend

in the pent-house of the liberated hotel
   Hang _up_ and dial again

This too a putrid placenta
   fouling the womb
   corrupting the vagina


III


Nations and people
   living on the edge of a death wish
   living by the law of the knife
   living upon the pinnacle of the sword

Do we smelter the branding iron
   Do we resurrect the Swastica
   Do we sear the flesh of the bicept
   the forehead or the buttock
   Or do we break out the genitals
   and wire them with electrodes
   Or save this sophisticated operation
   for the brain alone
   _When_ did we say yesterday
   was not tomorrow
At the edge of a death wish
   Centred in tall pyramids
   of plunder
   The heart cut out or else the tongue
   under the livid sky
   A purchase upon Cain's blood
   to negate the sign --
   are her thighs spread bare
   is the burden maim
Mr. Mumbo Jumbo is king crown
   Dr. King Craft is pax mundo
   Mr. Spike Tovarish
   has set up a boulevard of flag poles
   celebration Monday
   and the 4th of July
   Bulltoven my redeemable father

Death wish night a riot of no sound sleep
    Hoards of singing ancestors
    no melody in their cacophonous voices
    You have not been redeemed
    That black knife of timeless night
    has not shut out this restless pressure
    of questions and no answers
    You have not been redeemed
Drummers talked to me last night
    through a distant void
    They said to me, Mandrake
    are you the redeemer?
    I said, No--I am
    Bulltoven's hapless bastard
    though I have brothers

On the edge of a death wish
    My brother Baraka who might curse
    my name, as Mason would
    My brother Ché, who had the guts
    and had the cash
    Brother Mao, ancient of days
    who would fart loose a seam
    at the thought of it
And sisters too
    Theresa, my martyred saint
    My sister Angela, in LIFE magazine
    at ten, looking so nearly
    like my second daughter
    though believing in the law of the knife
    as survival's only way
    in which I cannot believe
I have survived until today
    And no knife in my hand
    nor in your own
    will vouchsafe my survival
    into tomorrow
    My darling sister still
    at Jacob's throne
Tania, my sister, the question is moot
    whether you collaborated
    in your own world's chaos

a whit more surely than
    one single other of the earth's wretched

Ultimately I will rest as you will
    on the edge of a bleak hill
    or a lush one
    my marker as simple as yours
I was circumcised at forty-three
    without an anaesthetic
    That was the day I learned
    a bullet may have the same power
    as a haiku
    to change the world
My dear brother
    Herbert Marcuse
    bless his <u>erotic</u> soul
    My sister, Bernadine Dohrn
    little sister of my heart's nurturance
Brother buzzard Ed, on the edge
    of a quiet desert, I salute you
    with your lame mare
    and your new bride
Distance, you might say
    is ever a handmaiden
    to brotherhood
    or else Bulltoven
    and his hapless brood

The death lash edging the darkness of dreams
    Awkward actors with putty fingers
    Equating studhood with statehood
    Equating condoms with genocide
    Belly-bloated women burning
    with starvation's fever
    Belly-bloated babies moaning
    with  starvation's fever
Tums for the tummy
    Water-logged ideologies
    smuggling gunpowder over
    torturous trails
    in creeping caravans
    through the whipping rain

Repeat again
    in the glaring beam of the searchlight

Repeat again
   out of the darkness
Repeat again
   in the moving shadows
Death wish
   The tension of nerves to be ready
   the slow wait
   Hot July
   ball busting broads
   September
   perched under a bridge-head with
   thirty-seven sticks of dynamite and
   a wilderness of wires
   My acheing groin

Or the edge of death's sweet smell
   The canvas cairn
   and his purchased father
   The king gander gain
   his flayed brother
   The maggot to her belly given
   though sprouting wings
   Talcum powder suffusing her ravenous vagina
   Princess of justice, mistress of swords

Living on the edge of a death wish
   The whisps of hemp where they
   left hanging
   The stroke of dawn where the
   plunder sweltered
   The handers of laurels gave
   the gunmen crowns
   The gunmen said "Gracias"
   and gunned them down
   The children fetched coppers
   to cover their eyes

IV

Nations and people
   Teetering on the brink of death's choice
      and devastation's volition

Your painted ass-holes with the paint
    flaked and cracking
    Your bloated eyelids
    with the corners pussy
    and festering
Oh,  the reincarnation of
    the day of victory
    with the corpses piled thick
    and the maggots feasting
Your name is Mammon
    alias the one party system
    Your fingers are crooked and
    contorted with greed
     Your swollen mouth is slovering
    with a hunger for power
    Your ugly genitals are flaccid
    with missuse
The rainbow of your promise
    has solidified into
    a never-ending shackle
    of tyranny
    Mammon is your final
    cursed name

The foul afterbirth
    clogging the womb
    engorging the vagina
    hanging in festoons
    like green snot
    from out the vagina
    poisoning the earth's milk
    the mother's breast
    This is the heritage of the law of the knife
    here is the height of the sword's pinnacle
    death wish home

Nations and people
    living by the law of the knife
    living upon the pinnacle of the sword

I would hector your peaceful
    slumber of dog night

the  shattered crystals of your
wish world palace
will rain down its thunder
upon the end of everything
your lying teeth have spoken
into crooked,  careening
pyramids of brutal power
I would hector the sword pinnacle
of your waking wish-fuck
catapulting the chest-raking
bone-rotting death to your
strong enemies and
to your weak friends
and to the wailing infant with
its bloated belly
wailing into your slumber
I would hector the putrid placenta
fouling the womb of nations
corrupting the cunt of continents
I would hector you your singular
dreams of high glory
corrupting the heart of power
at its moment of widest waking
and deepest wishing

This is the putrid placenta
fouling the belly
corrupting the vagina

Living on the edge of a death wish
This is where it ended
and not where it began
This is where the fell of blue steel
heeded no cry for tender mercy
This is where the spiked boots clicked
to each impending order
This is where the fang was
mechanical and potent
This is where the river left it
and will not return
This is where the talcumed butt
rolled over and wept

blind tears for a barren tomorrow
This is where the beath wish
fullfilled its name

CODA

Black and white is not
the true scar of our wounding
but ruler and ruined
the blood from that wound
is one colour and the hurt
when the mask sheds its spirit
no music, no strings

The wound with maggots--
the mind does not give blood
it does not give today or tomorrow
it is where the mask has shed
its spirit of strings naked
ruled, and the drum is silent

River and forest in mystical wound
paying six pints of red blood
for some light in front of
the ruled's blank face apank clean
with the dead mask and strings quiet
this animal is stalking still
at twilight his pads red
with that blood maggot gorged

Vanity has sucked all sap
from the spirit of preterknowing
bursting bellies, chests that grin
a fragment of dawn at sundown
the pain sucking the cods
in a tangled knob, betrayer
ruled, by the betrayed ruled

Judson Crews<br>
Lusaka, Zambia<br>
May 1974

$1.25

Cherry Valley Editions
Box 303
Cherry Valley,
N. Y. 13320